Respect

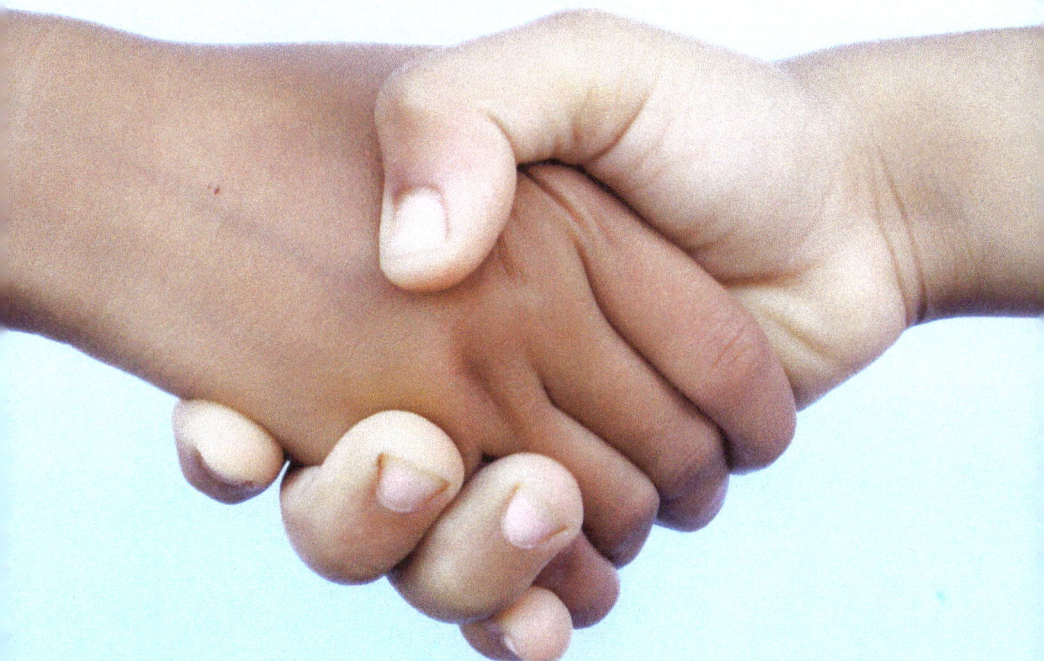

Ashley Lee

Explore other books at:
WWW.ENGAGEBOOKS.COM

VANCOUVER, B.C.

e →WWW.ENGAGEBOOKS.COM

Respect: Good Character Traits
Lee, Ashley, 1995 –
Text © 2025 Engage Books
Design © 2025 Engage Books

Edited by: A.R. Roumanis
Design by: Mandy Christiansen

Text set in Myriad Pro Regular.
Chapter headings set in Anton.

FIRST EDITION / FIRST PRINTING

LIBRARY AND ARCHIVES CANADA CATALOGUING IN PUBLICATION

Title: Respect / Ashley Lee.
Names: Lee, Ashley, author.
Description: Series statement: Good Character Traits

ISBN 978-1-77878-726-3 (hardcover)
ISBN 978-1-77878-732-4 (softcover)

This project has been made possible in part
by the Government of Canada. | Canada [🍁]

Respect

Contents

What Is Respect?

Respect means treating others the way you want to be treated.

It means showing kindness and thinking about other people's feelings.

Respect does not mean you always have to agree with others.

Why Is Respect Important?

Respect helps people build strong and caring friendships.

It creates a world where everyone feels **valued**.

What Does Respect Look Like?

Respectful people listen when others talk.

They use kind words and make sure no one feels **excluded**.

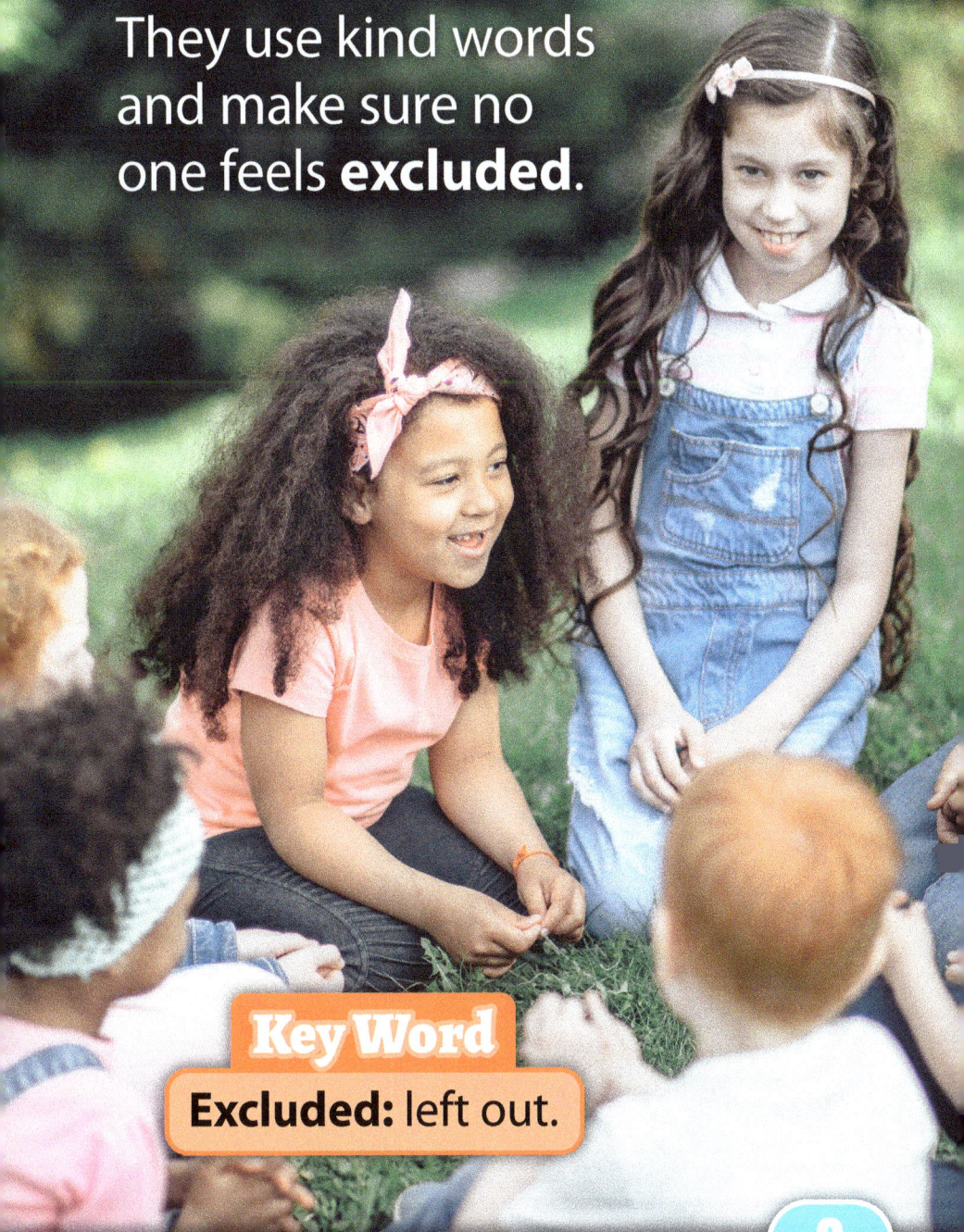

Key Word

Excluded: left out.

How Does Respect Affect You?

Being respectful makes you feel good about yourself.

It helps you become a friend that others can **trust**.

Key Word

Trust: the feeling that someone is there for you and believes in you.

How Does Respect Affect Others?

Being respected makes others feel important.

They know you care about them and their **opinions**.

Key Word

Opinions: what someone thinks or believes about something.

Does Everyone Respect Others?

Most people try to respect others. But sometimes people forget.

Having a lot of strong feelings can make people forget to be respectful.

It is important to say sorry if you forget to respect someone.

Is It Bad if You Do Not Respect Others?

Forgetting to show respect does not make you a bad person.

Say sorry, learn from your mistake, and try to show respect next time.

Does Respect Change Over Time?

Many people become more respectful as they get older.

They learn that being respectful often means they will be respected too.

Is It Hard to Respect Others?

It can be hard to respect someone if you are upset or do not agree with them.

Showing respect gets easier with **practice**.

Key Word

Practice: do something over and over again so you get better at it.

How Can You Learn to Be More Respectful?

Think about how your actions might affect others.

Think about how you would want to be treated if you were someone else.

How Can You Help Others Be More Respectful?

Be a **role model** to others by always respecting them.

Tell others how you feel when they do not respect you.

Tell a trusted adult if someone is not respectful over and over again.

How to Be Respectful Every Day

1. Listen when others are talking.

2. Use kind words

3. Share
and
take turns.

4. Do not
exclude
others.

Respect Around the World

People all over the world respect **cultures** they are not a part of.

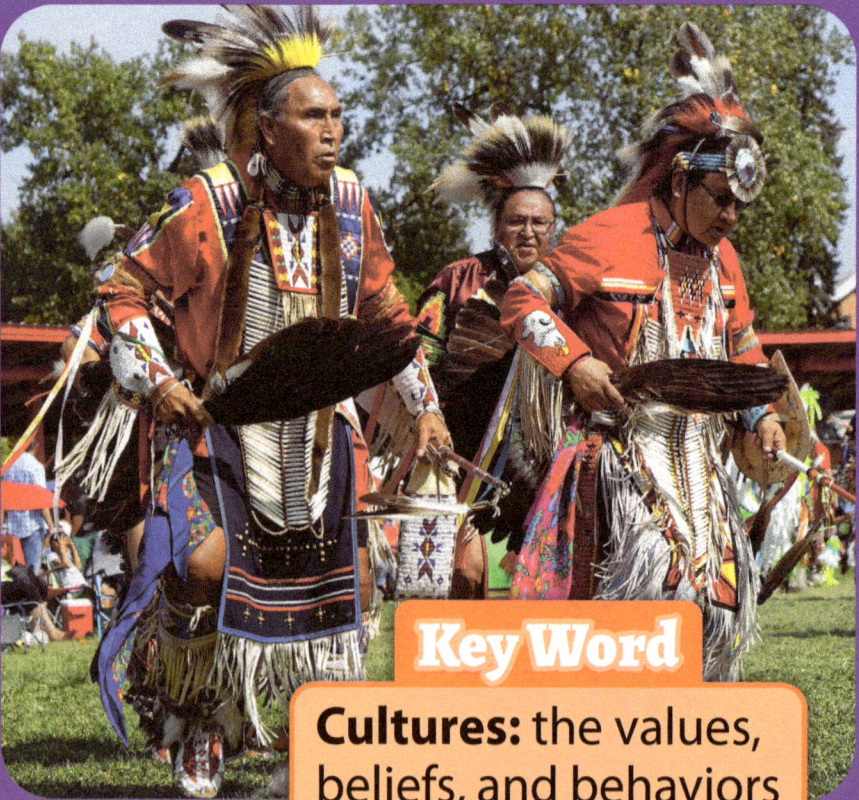

Key Word

Cultures: the values, beliefs, and behaviors of a group of people.

They do not put others down just because they do things differently.

Quiz

Test your knowledge of respect by answering the following questions. The questions are based on what you have read in this book. The answers are listed on the bottom of the next page.

1 Does respect help build strong and caring friendships?

2 Do respectful people listen when others talk?

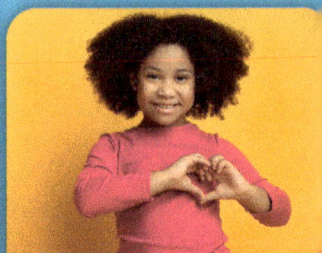

3 Does being respectful make you feel good about yourself?

4 Is it important to say sorry if you forget to respect someone?

5 Can it be hard to respect someone if you are upset or do not agree with them?

6 Should you tell others how you feel when they do not respect you?

Explore Other Level 1 Readers.

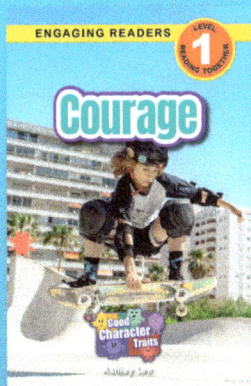
ENGAGING READERS — LEVEL 1 READING TOGETHER
Courage
Good Character Traits
Ashley Lee

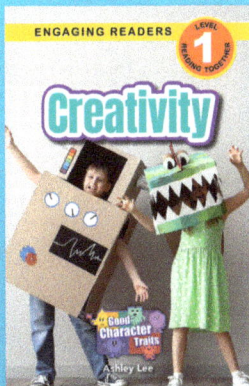
ENGAGING READERS — LEVEL 1 READING TOGETHER
Creativity
Good Character Traits
Ashley Lee

ENGAGING READERS — LEVEL 1 READING TOGETHER
Positivity
Good Character Traits
Ashley Lee

ENGAGING READERS — LEVEL 1 READING TOGETHER
Resilience
Good Character Traits
Ashley Lee

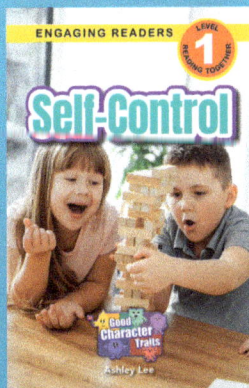
ENGAGING READERS — LEVEL 1 READING TOGETHER
Self-Control
Good Character Traits
Ashley Lee

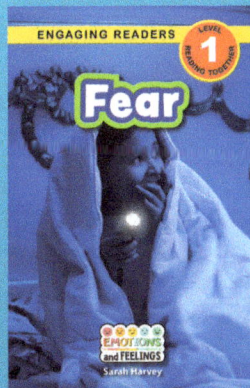
ENGAGING READERS — LEVEL 1 READING TOGETHER
Fear
EMOTIONS and FEELINGS
Sarah Harvey

ENGAGING READERS — LEVEL 1 READING TOGETHER
Happiness
EMOTIONS and FEELINGS
Sarah Harvey

ENGAGING READERS — LEVEL 1 READING TOGETHER
Sadness
EMOTIONS and FEELINGS
Sarah Harvey

ENGAGING READERS — LEVEL 1 READING TOGETHER
Surprise
EMOTIONS and FEELINGS
Sarah Harvey

Visit www.engagebooks.com/readers

www.ingramcontent.com/pod-product-compliance
Lightning Source LLC
Chambersburg PA
CBHW052036030426
42337CB00027B/5032